The Law of Attraction Series

DECIDE!

Book 1

VR Hogan

Copyright © 2019 VR Hogan
All rights reserved
First Edition

PAGE PUBLISHING, INC.
New York, NY

First originally published by Page Publishing, Inc. 2019

ISBN 978-1-68456-364-7 (Paperback)
ISBN 978-1-68456-365-4 (Digital)

Printed in the United States of America

Once you make a "decision," the universe conspires to make it happen.

—*Ralph Waldo Emerson*

It is my sincerest desire to write this book to be of service to my fellow human beings. The work put forth here is a labor of love. I am writing this book because I know that I can help others who want to produce better results from the efforts they have put in thus far. Though I am writing a book filled with ancient wisdom, I am however presenting this to you as one who is just like you. Yes, I have a great grasp for the law of attraction and its workings, and I could, and quite frankly, have taught this knowledge in some capacity. But in truth, I'm just like you. I'm presenting this work to you in the spirit of breaking the law of attraction and its workings down into a simple, plain English style. I'm not trying to insult anyone's intelligence when I say that but simply want to take the "mystical" tint off of the subject, so as to bring home the point that it's what "you" do all the time. Just like Bruce Lee did when he created Jeet Kune Do, he observed that the traditional martial arts had lots of unnecessary movements, thus the creation of the arts, which more than a few now practice even forty-plus years after his death. It is in this spirit that this series of books is written with this being the first.

Are you one of the many who've read the *Secret* by Rhonda Byrne or *The Law of Attraction* by Esther and Jerry Hicks? Or have you listened to a lot of YouTube videos featuring well-known teachers of the law of attraction such as Bob Proctor or Lisa Nichols to name a few? Are you one of the people who have gone so far as paying hundreds of dollars to attend seminars to learn about the law and its workings? More importantly, are you one of the people who've done one or more of the above-mentioned activities and yet still ask the question, "Why is the law of attraction *not* working for me?" If the answer to this question is *yes*, then this book is just for you. In fact, it's the law of attraction that has led you here. This book will show you not only why you haven't gotten the results you think you should've gotten, but that you're actually responsible for what you've gotten thus far. This book isn't intended to show you any magic tricks or special formulas. It's more a book to give you a pat on the back and let you know that you're actually doing a great job; and if you would only do this one thing correctly, you'd get the results you really wanted and not just get what you've get by default. So if you've been trying to manifest the life you want but still not happy with the results you've produced or just simply don't understand how you've done what you've done, then I invite you to dive in as this book will simplify what has somehow been made complicated. If you really want to have more love in your life, better relationships, more time for the things that matter most to you, more money, a better job or career, or better overall health, then this book is just for you.

My goal is that when you finish reading these works, you will feel a weight lifted off of your shoulders and have a renewed enthusiasm toward life. I wish for you to not only see the beauty I see in life, but to also understand that this is an exciting time to be alive. I intend that you be empowered by knowing that you are right where you need to be at this time in your life and that everything that you've gone through—good, bad, or indifferent—was to set you up for the success you are now primed to enjoy.

I want you to know up front that these are not books of great length, and that though not long, the material herein is powerful, but not because I wrote them, but because they are *you*, and that I am your servant in this instant. I would also like to say that though I will use the word *God* in these books that these are not religious works. I am in no way condemning anybody's beliefs or faith as it is my view that there is only one spiritual teaching, and that it simply takes many different forms. I will for the most part point to the fact of how powerful you were born to be and that the time is *now* to claim your birthright.

With that said, ladies and gentlemen, I am humbled and honored to present book one of the law of attraction and its workings…DECIDE!

CHAPTER 1

Though the law of attraction is as old as time itself, it has only become a popular subject within the last decade or so. With the *Secret* hitting the scene in 2006 as well as *The Law of Attraction* by Esther and Jerry Hicks, people have not only watched the movie and read the books, but have more importantly put the law into action, sometimes though, not to the effect that they would've liked. I have often been approached by people with the question "Why doesn't the law of attraction work like I want it to?" I get this question from people wherever I go. People actually ask me this question and don't even know they're asking it sometimes. I've gotten this question not only from people I know, but from total strangers. Talk about the law of attraction! Though I get this question from both friends and strangers, I think it only fair to let you know that the question was asked mostly of me by me.

    I first got wind of the law via the *Secret* like most people I know. Once I saw it, I was hooked! I wasn't only out to manifest what I wanted. I wanted to know everything there was to know about the law of attraction. I not only read and watched the *Secret* multiple times, I also went to the *Secret's* website and read the suggested reading, two ebooks in particular that the site offers for free, *The Master Key System* by Charles F. Haanel and *The Science of Getting Rich* by Wallace D. Wattles, both of which have been instrumental in my understanding of just what the law is all about. I was one who went about every spare moment I had to get more and more information about the subject. I watched numerous videos on YouTube of Abraham (Esther Hicks) and Bob Proctor among others, and I have numerous audiobooks on the subject as well. Inevitably, I grew tired of watching videos and reading all of the time. I wanted put what I'd learned into action. As I set out to put the law to the test, I noticed that I wasn't getting the results I thought I should be getting. I thought to myself, I've done all of this research and studying, but where I was at that time wasn't where I thought I should be. What the crap, I thought! Is this it? Was all the information I took in a bunch of lies? However, I knew the basic tenant of the law, which is you attract to yourself what you focus on the most. But then, my question was, is this what I am focusing on? How the hell am I attracting this? Though I wasn't getting what I thought should be getting, I did however realize that the knowledge of the law of attraction came to me for a reason, and it wasn't to deceive or mislead me, so I kept at it, as if I had a choice. As I mentioned before, once I watched the *Secret*, I was hooked. If I know anything in life, it's this. If I "really" want to know something, it will come to me. It may not come right away, but when it does, I recognize it for what it is, and that's exactly what happened to get me past the sticking point of why I wasn't getting the results I desired.

The reason I wasn't getting the results I wanted and the reason you aren't getting the results you want is a very simple one. If you're still not getting the results you want, it's simply because you haven't made a *decision*. That is to say, you aren't clear on what it is you really want. I know, I can already hear you saying, like I did once upon a time, "But I wanted this but I got that!? How did that happen?" Well, let me explain it like this. You actually need to understand that the law of attraction is *you*. Not just something you use when you want something and then you just go back to what you were doing, and then when you want something again, you activate the law. No, I tell you that is a mistake of epic proportions if you want to get what you want and not just simply what you get. Understand this, the law is always working. It's just a matter of being conscious of it to make it do what you "want" as opposed to it giving you what you've focused on the most, which may not be to your liking. You see, the missing link that I wasn't getting is, you're manifesting at every moment. It's really an issue of do you know what you are manifesting. By this I mean, the universe gives you what you focus on the most, the only question that remains is, what are you focusing on and are you conscious of that focus?

The reason I decided to name this book DECIDE is because of a quote that I came across from a fellow author a couple of days ago. The quote said this: "Genocide is killing a group of people, homicide is killing one person, suicide is to kill oneself, but to *decide* is to kill every other option!" At the time I decided to write this book, I didn't really have a title or direction for what I was going to write for that matter, I just knew it would be about the law of attraction; but when I saw the above quote, I knew right away what the title of this book would be. It just made perfect sense. In most literature concerning the law of attraction, you hear it's what we focus on most that manifests in our reality; but if you think about it, it really comes down to making a decision. We make decisions all the time but are mostly oblivious to them.

When you consider that we are primarily discussing the question of why the law hasn't worked as you maybe would've liked, you should accept and understand that the law is always working. There is never a time that it is not, it's that simple. I came to this realization recently. I now say that "the *Secret* is not a secret, it's brilliant marketing." The only thing that's a secret is that you've been doing everything the *Secret* is talking about, it's just a matter of you being conscious of it?" You get what you get and not what you want simply because you're not making a conscious decision.

I would say that you're not focusing but that would technically be incorrect because as I just pointed out, you're always manifesting something whether you know it or not, so there has to be some form of focusing going on. But when you decide or make a decision about something, it says that you're consciously focusing, not just remote control focusing. A decision locks in on what you want rather than just leaving things to chance, which if you think about it, is why the question of why am I not manifesting what I want is being asked so often.

In my search to learn more about the law and its workings, I've discovered that there are actually seven steps to manifesting what you want. That said, this book will only focus on the first step of the seven. This is not to say that the other six aren't important, that's far from the case, but if you want to manifest what you really want, then you'll need to master the first step.

As I alluded to a little earlier, you're always manifesting something, but are you consciously doing it or are you doing it by default? I also said that I would let you know that you were already doing a great job despite you not having what you wanted, so that is exactly what I'm doing right now. I do however need to make this point clear on two fronts. Point one, please understand that you're manifesting at *all times*. Always have and always will for that matter. Second, I know that if you are reading this book, then you're like me. You've read and studied lots of material on the subject and have been trying to put what you've learned into action. The great news is, *you're actually succeeding!* Yes. You've been succeeding. Congratulations! I know what you must be saying. How am I a success if I don't have what I've been trying to get? Well it's like this, and I know this may sound a little contradictive; but if you stay with me, it'll all make sense. Yes, you need to make a decision, and for the most part a lot of you have. The real "gold" here is to understand what's actually taking place when you do make a decision, whether it's conscious or not.

CHAPTER 2

As I know you are a student of the law of attraction, whether you realize it or not, I can safely assume you've heard the phrase "Everything is mind." With that, the next step would be to know how the mind works. It's not complicated at all, and here it is. There are two parts of the mind, the conscious mind and the subconscious mind. The conscious mind is what you're making your decision with. Once you've made up your mind as to what you want, the subconscious mind then takes over. The subconscious mind is actually your connection to the universal mind, or source if you would. The subconscious is what actually does the manifesting. Whatever your conscious mind takes hold of or focuses on "predominately" is what your subconscious mind manifests. The subconscious does not argue with the conscious mind, in fact, it's indiscriminate. When you recognize this fact, you now understand how you get what you want or simply what you get. To bring home the second point, yes you've done a great job of putting the law into action; it's just that you don't recognize what it looks like in your life.

Often people put what they've learned to the test and don't immediately see (with their physical eyes) what they think they should. But in reality, understanding what I've pointed out about the conscious or finite mind being the decision maker and the subconscious mind being what manifests what you want, as it is your connection to the universal or infinite mind, you can then see that the infinite mind has started moving in your favor. The lack of seeing what you want in no way means that the law hasn't worked. In fact, we were put here to make decisions so that the universe can manifest things through us and carry out its intended overall purpose. Thing is, you need to recognize that the finite mind sees or perceives things from a certain view, which is somewhat limited. The infinite mind has what you might call a bird's eye view. In the physical, you simply see what you want, the object if you would, but the infinite mind sees the "how" of it and starts things moving in the right direction for you.

The problem that occurs is that when we don't see what we want, we give up and think we've done something incorrectly, when in fact we were doing a *beautiful* job but just simply failed to recognize what we'd set in motion with our decisions. So, you either give up and settle back into getting what we get or find something else you think you want or can get and start again. And with that, the universe says OK and curtails what it was previously doing, as you are the boss and it does what you tell it to. All the while, you were doing a great job and didn't even know it. When I realized what I was doing, and this after numerous attempts at trying to get what I wanted, I felt so good because I recognized that after all of the perceived mishaps that I "thought" I was having, that it was not only not as bad as it seemed, but that I was closer than I thought. It was both a relief and reaffirming to me that it was all in my hands to not only change my reality, but also that the shortcomings were correctable. Though I felt like giving up, in my heart I knew that wasn't an option.

CHAPTER 3

When you consciously decide what you want, you'll start to notice things happening. You'll begin to notice the right people will start gravitating toward you. I am a perfect example of how making a decision will start a chain reaction of people and events transpiring to bring said decision to fruition. The fact that you are reading this book is a testament to this. Let me illuminate how it has worked for me. I have an internet radio talk show that I've been doing for approximately three years now. I've formatted the show a few different ways over that time so that I could cover a broad list of topics that I enjoy talking about and researching. Most recently, I've been doing two days a week with the two days covering differing topics. I scheduled a Friday night session to cover the topics that just seem to gravitate toward me like spiritual physics, the law of one, the Book of Enoch, human origins, and the secret doctrine just to name a few. My Sunday show covers anything having to do with the law of attraction. I had absolutely no problems talking about the law of attraction because as I stated earlier, once I got wind of it, I was hooked. My journey has basically been all about finding out everything I could about the law and its working, so that came out quite naturally, but as for the subject matter for my Friday show, that's another story. Though I have a grasp for what I wanted to cover, conveying the information to a listening audience is another matter. Due to scheduling conflicts and inconsistencies, I, in a sense, lost my direction over a period of a few months. That said, I addressed my audience one night and told them that I was going to discontinue the Friday night session because I didn't feel as if I was doing a great job communicating what I wanted to communicate to them. I told them that I thought that I would be better served putting all of that knowledge in a book. As soon as I made the "decision" to write a book, things immediately started moving me in the direction that would pave the way for me to do just that.

I received emails inviting me to join a fiction challenge. The beauty of this challenge is that it taught me valuable information about the intricacies of the writing a book. What I've actually failed to mention, by the way, is even before I started my radio talk show, I wanted to write books. I just didn't know what it entailed. As a matter of fact, when I actually made the decision to write, it was exactly one year to the day that I'd taken the time to sit down and write down some goals that I would like to accomplish. Truth is, I'd been trying to write a book since December 2014, but for reasons I need not go into here, I just didn't get it done. Once I made the declaration that I would put what I wanted to communicate to my listening audience into a book, *viola*! Things started moving in my direction, and *immediately* at that!

As I said earlier, I'd wanted to write at least one book approximately sixteen months prior to the writing of the one you're reading now. I had a great idea going on inside my head for about two weeks, as I was looking forward to the Christmas break that year at the job I was working. There were two things that hindered my progress. First was the fact that I had no clue how I would go about getting the book out to the public. Secondly, I just didn't have the peace and quiet that I thought I would be enjoying over this ten-day break. I was living with my some family members that for some reason wanted to blast the radio all day and company was in and out all of the time. Not to mention the free loading relatives that were there doing whatever they thought they wanted to do as well (laughing as I'm writing this). I was so frustrated that I wouldn't get to write that book because I had some *great* material floating around in my head. That said, I went on with my life as it was going. Now, I do want to point out that I did make the "decision" to write a book back then, but if that be the case, why am I just now writing a book nearly two years later? If the statement that opens this book by Ralph Waldo Emerson is true, why didn't the universe move as swiftly then as it did now?

Well actually it did. I know that may sound confusing, but stay with me, it'll all make sense in a moment. Yes, I did make the decision to write a book, one that would look a lot different from this one. In the earlier paragraph, I said that when I announced to my listening audience that I would put the content I wanted to communicate to them into book form and events started to transpire to that effect. Well one of the tools the universe used to point me in the right direction hadn't come into my possession yet. Two days after I'd made the declaration on my show I received an email via a program that I joined through Facebook approximately six months prior to then looking to point myself in the direction of writing, which was about nine months after my failed attempt to write over the Christmas 2014 holiday. The program wasn't what I thought it was but as there was no monthly payment involved, I still glanced at the emails as they came in every once in a while for anything that might be useful. They would post different writing jobs, but I wasn't interested in those at the time, but the email I got two days later was an invitation to join a Kindle fiction challenge. I looked into it and decided that I wanted to join. Now I can already hear you saying, how is a "fiction challenge" relevant to you making a decision to write the book I'm now reading, and it's a nonfiction book at that?" Great question actually. Before I explain how it worked, I would like you to keep in mind that the universe didn't just move immediately like I previously mentioned. It was *always* moving on my behalf, even when I thought I failed at writing over the Christmas 2014 break. Even before I joined the previously mentioned writers program, about six months prior to that I went to a local Starbucks and began to write out some goals and things that I wanted to manifest in my life. One of the things that I wrote was that I wanted to take all of the knowledge that I studied and instead of putting it into a nonfiction book, I would craft it into a fictional tale. This was March 22, 2015. A little more than six months later on September 24, 2015, I joined the writing service. It was March 11, 2016, when I announced to my listening audience that I would put the knowledge in book form.

Now there is a distinct difference at each end of this example. In the first instance, I wanted to write a book, and badly. The thing is I only wanted to write the book. I hadn't really decided to. Yes, I daydreamed about it. I was excited with anticipation looking forward to the time off that I would do it, but I hadn't decided to do it. I didn't have that "I'm going to get it done no matter what" attitude that I have now. In fact, at that time I pretty much felt as if the universe was conspiring against me. It was one of those "Oh this is an impossible coincidence" type of feelings. I was a little frustrated but nothing that depressed me. To put further emphasis on the point I'm making, when I decided to write, I actually hit what you might call a financial land mine! That's right. Again, it was one of those "You've got to be kidding me" type of deals. I was doing great one minute and asking what the hell the next. It looked as if the same thing was happening all over again, like the universe was conspiring against me, but when I didn't panic and simply recognized what was going on, I started to see how things were moving in the direction of my decision.

Here's what happened. Remember when I spoke about joining the Kindle fiction challenge? Well normally I would've been able to pay for that without blinking so much as an eye, but when I hit the financial land mine, I had just enough to pay for my living arrangements, my phone bill, transportation to work, and for my sustenance, with little leftover for the other necessities of everyday life. When I received the email announcing the fiction challenge, I just simply didn't have the funds available to me to join. Again, I didn't panic. Remember, I made a *decision*, and when you do that, the universe conspires to make it happen. Well right in the nick of time, someone walked up to me at work with a check for $400. A bonus that I'd been told I wasn't going to get actually. I'd forgotten all about it. Even though I wanted to join the fiction challenge (which by the way was nowhere near $400 to join) but had no surplus income to do it, I recalled something from Robert Kiyosaki's *Rich Dad, Poor Dad*. In that book he said, "Don't say I can't afford something. Instead ask how can I afford it?" With that attitude, I stayed calm and didn't attempt to force anything. Then the day that the challenge started *bang*! My supervisor walked up to me with a check, but that was only the beginning. Joining that fiction challenge was only a stepping stone to me writing this particular book. Believe me when I say, I have some great fiction coming your way in the near future, but the reason this book is in existence is because of something I came across as soon as I joined the challenge. You're reading this book because of something that the group leader suggested. She suggested I joined Geoff Shaw's Kindling program. In joining Kindling, I not only got the know how to get my book out to the public, I'm now in touch with so many other people that have had the same dreams and desires as me. I went from not having a clue to being able to simply ask a question on a closed Facebook group to get any help I may need. That's a far cry from me just looking forward to some off time so that I could write a book that I had no idea how to get published. So you see, when it looked as if the universe was conspiring against me, but in actuality, it was working on my behalf, even back then.

CHAPTER 4

So what decisions are you actually making? When we consider the subject of manifesting, we normally think of material things, but the truth of the matter is that we are manifesting much more than that. As a matter of fact, it is one of the reasons why we've incarnated into this life. With that said, we often get caught up in the everyday flow of life. We actually think that the lives we live are "it." This is far from the truth. Yes, we find ourselves living what we call lives but it's a little more involved than we realize. When making the decisions we make, most of the time we fail to recognize that it's not even us that are making the decisions most of the time. If you were to take an inventory of the decisions you've made over a period of time, you'd more than likely see that at least some of the choices you've made are at best questionable. There may be some things that you look back on and ask yourself, "Why the hell did I do that? Or what was I thinking?" A good portion of the decisions we make are influenced by a number of factors. We are influenced by our ancestry, our environment, the things we see on television and listen to on the radio, what the people around us say, just to name a few, but the real beauty of what this book is actually all about is that no matter what decisions you've made in the past, the power to change it lays totally within your grasp. All you have to do is *make the decision*, but again, what decisions are you making?

    Well a good place to start is to examine the question first posed in this book. Why isn't the law working for me like I want it to? I mentioned that the law works all of the time and that we actually do a great job, but that we don't necessarily recognize what we've done. Truth be told, we should understand another factor at play. Ask yourself this question: What am I saying to myself? This requires that you really understand *you*. By that I mean get to know your own inner self. Start to notice how you think about things or how you talk about things. For that matter, start taking inventory of the people around you. How they talk, what they believe, their general mindset. This is important as you'll start to see what it is you're attracting to yourself, or more importantly, you will start seeing a reflection of yourself. Remember, you don't attract what you like, you attract what you *are*. Once you do that, start putting together what you think about and how you talk coupled with what your environment or reality are showing you.

As with most of us, when the law of attraction became popular, we for the most part wanted to manifest material things. Speaking from experience, I printed out the blank check from the *Secret*'s website and promptly filled it out with my first, middle, and last name, along with the amount of $10,000. Let me just say that that was back in 2009. It's now 2018 as I write this. I only mention this because I have never received a check of $10,000 or anything close to that amount for that matter. I am quite sure that that amount and more has come into my possession since that time, but if I'm honest, I wrote the check out for that amount to come at one time, not over the period of nine years. So the question becomes, what happened? I can explain it this way, I made the decision with the intention to get $10,000 somehow, as I took the time to print the blank check and fill it out as I did, but I actually didn't make the decision from a totally conscious perspective.

When I pose the question of "So what decisions are we actually making," I'm really speaking more to the "unconscious" decisions that we make by default. In the example I've offered here, I outline the steps that should be taken in such a case, but there is an underlying reason that after nine years that I don't have that check…yet. When you really examine the situation, you may find that there may be an issue with how I think about money. When I wrote the amount of $10,000 dollars out, why did I write that amount? Was it because I finally saw an opportunity to get more money than I'd ever had at one time in my life? Or did I really have a reason for wanting that much money? Maybe I wanted to start a business or expand a business? Perhaps I wanted to pay off a debt? No matter what the answer, one thing is recognized, I never received the amount I settled on.

I can tell you however that after careful examination of how I think about things, when I wrote that check I didn't think like a person who thought they would get a check for that amount. I didn't, at that time, know what I'd even do with $10,000. I didn't prepare like I knew it was coming my way. I just simply settled on having $10,000. What I would do with it, I didn't even have a clue. So is the possibility of a $10,000 check out of the question, even after so much time has passed? The short answer is *no*. I mention this example as this book is so much more than a simple manifestation manual. It is a book that not only speaks to the ancient wisdom of the law, but more so a testament to real-life applications. When we make decisions, even conscious ones, the results may not be as fast as we'd like. This doesn't mean that what we've decided on is a dead stick. There are factors that go into the why we would even make said decision to begin with. There are certain beliefs that we hold that may hinder how the things we've decided on come into concrete form. We may believe that what we want will take a certain amount of time, but this may not be the way it "actually" is according to the universe. Often, the decisions we make are not bold, but somewhat calculated. You see, we don't usually make the larger than life decisions we "really" desire as we often don't think we can get it, though everything in the universe is already yours. We too often submit to what our five senses are telling us. What our environment is telling us. What our family and friends are saying.

One thing that goes largely unrecognized is that when we have visions of grandeur, were those visions to become reality, what our lives would look like may be vastly different from how they appeared before the changes. As stated earlier, we do a *great* job of manifesting our realities, but once the changes start to manifest, as we are now more conscious of what we've always done, we become frightened due to the unexpected changes of what we've done. Yes, we have the ability to manifest the reality we really want, especially in this day and age, but it is vitally important to understand this: you must become the person that that success belongs to. When you wish to manifest something, it's more than a simple matter of getting something. Understand that when the universe conspires to bring what we want to us, you may be faced with the hard choice of leaving what has been a comfort for us. It may mean parting ways with people who you actually love but are not in the best interest of what it is we really want.

In the example I shared about the $10,000 check, if I'd have actually gotten that at that time, I believe that it would have attracted more stress than elation. In the environment that I was in at that time, I was around people who had what might be called a poverty consciousness, not to mention that I myself was still of that state of mind, which more than likely contributed to why the check has yet to manifest. It happens all the time, someone gets a large sum of money and then *bam*! All of a sudden, people who you never knew start coming out of the woodworks, acting friendly, being insincere, and everything that comes along with it. Now that I'm manifesting what I want, I am in a better situation to be a wise steward over the blessings that I am bestowed with.

CHAPTER 5

Probably the biggest hindrance to getting what we want is us trying to tell the universe how to do its job. The one lesson that sticks out the most from my study of the *Secret* is that the "what" is our job, not the "how." We come up with good ideas, but we too often try to force the issue as to how they become manifest. Whenever you hear of people saying they want a mate, they feel the desire true enough, but then as soon as something "looks" promising, you often see that they rush in headlong, falsely thinking that this must be what the universe sent me. In truth, it's more akin to hoping, as the results of most situations are not as satisfactory to the initial intention. If one were to do an honest study of the example offered here, the results would more than likely resemble the divorce rates of today of around 75 percent. This is not to say that most marriages or relationships are destined to fail. I am simply pointing out how the power to manifest the lives we want will always go wrong when the inherent power we possess is incorrectly used. Rest assured that there are people who have found real, lasting happiness in this area of their lives as well as others areas, but with this being a book about the real life applications of the law it's important that I point out what's getting in the way of manifesting what we really want.

As I've pointed out numerous times thus far that we are doing a magnificent job even though we are not getting what we want. The intent is to show that the wisdom here attached is not just from some guru that you'll see on Oprah or even on YouTube. It is my truest desire to communicate with you as someone who is just like you. With that said, most of what is being put forth in this book is not so much about the proper way of doing things, as that is well documented. This is a tell-all of sorts to show what we've for the most part been doing wrong or, more accurately, what we've unconsciously done. We get what we get and not what we want as we are not consciously conscious. The great news about this is that we are in a place in the evolution of mankind where we are rapidly awakening. You see, there is a reason that they say this wisdom was hidden or that it was a secret. Truth is that humanity wasn't in a place where it was ready to take advantage of it, which is really to say that we hadn't yet reached that point in our evolution of consciousness to even recognize it, though we were already doing it. Another way of looking at it would be to consider that our past shortcomings are actually a blessing as we now are in a position to recognize what we've done incorrectly and what adjustments we need to make.

If you consider that when we manifest something into our lives that it is not simply for the sake of having the thing or circumstance we want. There is a far greater dynamic involved here that most of us are unaware. I'm a fan of what the great Deepak Chopra says. He says that "God is static." This is to say that God is everywhere. There is no place that God is not present. The only thing that God cannot get away from is *itself*. We, humanity, are all a way of God getting away from *itself*, therefore the experiences that we have here on earth in fact are for God." So when we manifest anything into reality, we are acting in lieu of *God itself*. We are all individual sparks of the *whole*. When we are aligned with our highest vibrations or truest desire, we are in alignment with God, the God within us. When we now make conscious decisions or more accurately form a picture or visualize something, we can trust that whatever that may be is of the *divine*, thus you get what you want as opposed to simply getting what you get.

Another way to look at this would be to understand what Wallace Wattles says in his book *The Science of Getting Rich*." He quotes: "There is a thinking stuff, from which all things are made, which in its original form permeates, penetrates, and fills the inner spaces of the universe. A thought, in this substance, produces the thing imaged by the thought. Man can form things in his thought, and, by impressing his thought upon formless substance, cause the thing that he thinks about to be created."

Remember when I said that we are here as a way of God getting away from *itself*? Well, once you grasp the total concept of this statement, you start to recognize that all of the dreams that we've failed to realize have been due to our own misunderstanding of just what we are. We were simply unaware of just what and who we really are. We were where we were for a reason, but as there is a mass awakening happening even as we speak, we now recognize that everything was simply a preparatory phase for what we were destined to be at this juncture in the time space continuum.

When we understand this, the realization sets in that though we may have made decisions based on fear or lack or disbelief in the past, the future or present for that matter are far more brighter than we ever imagined. It is no longer a question of "whose I am" as in being a child of God, but an affirming *fact* of who you *are*. We can now take the training wheels off so to speak and take this beautiful thing we are out for a real joy ride.

Once you reconcile the ideas, dreams, visions, and hopes that you are inspired by on a daily basis are in fact God within coming out of you, you now see that you didn't decide to come to suffer. You didn't come to serve out a punishment for past lives. You decided to come here to be of service to humanity and by doing so become an extension of *God itself*. So you can rest assured that though it seemed you failed in the past, this is far from the case. Like the great Michael Jordan once said: "I'm only great because I failed so much." Even then, you haven't failed. You were just practicing and warming up. Realize that you are full of *great* ideas and that those ideas are actually God speaking from within you and then simply *decide* what you want.

Once you make a conscious decision, it'll be time to advance to the next step in the process…*desire*.

ABOUT THE AUTHOR

VR Hogan is an armed forces veteran born and raised in Detroit, Michigan. It is through his travels around the world that he has become a spiritual seeker and student of the law of attraction, as well as a proponent of ancient occult wisdom. The experiences of his journey have inspired him to be of service to the collective by becoming both an author and radio talk show host.

CPSIA information can be obtained
at www.ICGtesting.com
Printed in the USA
LVHW110754070920
665161LV00052B/897